GW00991975

CHRISTIA

BEFORE

CHRIST

▼

By

JOHN G. JACKSON

▼

Martino Publishing
Mansfield Centre, CT
2015

Martino Publishing
P.O. Box 373,
Mansfield Centre, CT 06250 USA

ISBN 978-1-61427-848-1

© *2015 Martino Publishing*

Cover design by T. Matarazzo

Printed in the United States of America On 100% Acid-Free Paper

CHRISTIANITY BEFORE CHRIST

By

JOHN G. JACKSON

THE BLYDEN SOCIETY
1890 SEVENTH AVENUE
NEW YORK, N.Y.

Christianity Before Christ....

St. Augustine, most celebrated of the African Fathers of the Church, admitted the origin of Christianity before the advent of the Christian savior. In his own words:

"The same thing which is now called Christian religion existed among the ancients. They have begun to call Christian the true religion which existed before."

THE Study of comparative religions in recent years has shown the truth of St. Augustine's contention.

Before, however, discussing the origins of the Christian religion, it is necessary that we examine its foundations. Definitions of Christianity are almost useless, owing to the fact that nearly every sect and denomination in Christendom has its own doctrine. The primitive Baptist and the conservative Unitarian both call themselves Christians, but the ideas of the two on the subject are poles apart. There are broadly speaking two schools of Christian thought, namely: Fundamentalism and Modernism. The Fundamentalists, or Orthodox Christians, are the majority party in the Church and base their religion on the authority of the Bible, which they regard as the word of God, a book which is true from cover to cover, and must be accepted as such by all good Christians. The Modernists, or liberal Christians, on the other hand, do not consider the Bible the word of God. And though they believe it contains truth, they admit that it also harbors myths, legends and errors. The modernists are vastly in the minority. Many modernists are so free in their interpretation of Christianity, that the orthodox have often accused them of being free from the religion altogether. But passing over these differences, it seems that in order to be considered a Christian, one must at least believe in the two cardinal doctrines of the Christian religion. Those doctrines are (1) the Fall of Man and (2) the Atonement. I have met people who call themselves Christians, who claim that they accept neither doctrine, but I never could fathom the logic of their mental processes. According to the doctrine of the Fall, man was created perfect by divine fiat, but due to the sin of Adam, mankind fell from "grace," and hence became a lost race. The Creator, according to Holy Writ, in due time, assumed human form and allowed himself to be slain for the salvation of humanity. This Atonement is of course a corrollary of the Fall. Had man never fallen it would of course never been necessary to save him. Among the orthodox, these doctrines are rightly considered dogmas, i.e., beliefs to be accepted without question. The liberal Christians, as a rule, accept the doctrine of evolution. They believe that man is descended from the so-called lower animals, that he is a cousin of the great apes and a remote relation to all the other forms of life. Since evolution teaches that man has risen, by Selection, Mutations, and Changes, and Genesis teaches just the opposite, it is difficult to see how one can believe in both the testimony of Geology and the testimony of Genesis at one and the same time. The orthodox claim, very logically, that if evolution is accepted, a litteral belief in the Fall, is impossible. As a result, belief in the Atonement would be absurd, since the only reason for accepting it has been abandoned. This point has been well put by T. W. Doane:

"These two dogmas cannot be separated from each other. If there was no Fall, there is no need of an atonement, and no Redeemer is required. Those, then who consent in recognizing in Christ Jesus a God and Redeemer, and who, notwithstanding, cannot resolve upon admitting the story of the Fall of man to be historical, should exculpate themselves from the reproach of inconsistency. There are a great number however, in this position at the present day."

Now that the foundations of Christianity have been sufficiently dealt with, we may proceed with the main argument. Anyone who is at all acquainted with the literature of social anthropology, especially the works of Sir James G. Frazer ("The Golden Bough", etc,), Edward Carpenter ("Pagan & Christian Creeds") and the Rt. Hon. J. M. Robertson ("Christianity & Mythology", etc.), knows of the numerous Pagan Christs, who lived or were supposed to have lived hundreds and thousands of years before the time of Jesus. The most famous of these pre-Christian divinities were Osiris and Horus of Egypt, Krishna and Buddha of India, Mithra of Persia, Quetzalcoatl of Mexico, Adonis of Babylonia, Bacchus of Greece and Attis of Phrygia. When we examine the traditions, myths and legends concerning these heathen gods, we find that their life stories follow a common pattern. They are, as a rule, said to have been born on or near December 25th, an approximation of the Winter Solstice (the beginning of winter), a holiday now known as Christmas. They are reputedly born of virgin mothers. Their nativity is almost invariably announced by a star. They are said to have been born in either a cave or a stable. They are represented as being slain, commonly by crucifixion, but not invariably so. At the time of their deaths, the sun is reported to have had its light blotted out. These slain saviors almost always, it is said, descend into Hell. They, as a rule, are pictured as rising from the dead, on or near March 25th, an approximniation of the vernal Equinox (the beginning of Spring), the holiday known to us as Easter.

Though it is not generally known, the ancient Egyptians worshipped, a virgin born savior, thousands of years before Christ. This Egyptian Christ, Horus, is one of the oldest Gods of Egypt. The Sphinx is a statue which was erected to his memory. The French Egyptologist, Prof. Hippolyte Boussac, holds that this great monument was carved out of solid rock at least 10,000 years ago. From the Edfu Text and the Ethiopian physiognomy of the Sphinx, we conclude that Horus was a pre-dynastic Ethiopian king, who was instrumental in introducing civilization into Egypt. He was eventually deified by the Egyptians, who identified him

with the sun-god. In the temples of ancient Egypt, the birthday of Horus was celebrated on or near December 25th. An image of him was displayed lying in a manger, since his birth is said to have occured in a stable. An image of his mother, the Virgin Isis, was shown standing by the manger. This same tableaux, with the infant Jesus and the Virgin Mary supplanting the infant Horus and the Virgin Isis, is presented in Catholic Churches on Christmas in our own day. The parallels between the religions of ancient Egypt and Christianity are so close that they warrant the attention of all serious students of history. This point is well expressed by the Rev. Professor John Pentland Mahaffy, who declares:

"There is indeed, hardly a great or fruitful idea in the Jewish or Christian systems, which has not its analogy in the ancient Egyptian faith. The development of the one God into a trinity; the incarnation of the mediating deity in a Virgin and without a father; his conflict and his momentary defeat by the powers of darkness, his partial victory (for the enemy is not destroyed); his resurrection and reign over an eternal kingdom with his justified saints; his distinction from, and yet identity with, the uncreate incomprehensible Father, whose form is unknown, and dwelleth not in temples made with hands—all these theological conceptions pervade the oldest religion of Egypt. So, too, the contrast and even the apparent inconsistencies between our moral and theological beliefs— the vacillating attribution of sin and guilt partly to moral weakness, partly to the interference of evil spirits, and likewise of righteousness to moral worth, and again to the help of good genii or angels; the immortality of the soul and its final judgment—all these things have met us in the Egyptian ritual and moral treatises. So, too, the purely human side of morals, and the catalogue of virtues and vices, are by natural consequences as like as, are the theological systems." ("Prolegomena to Ancient History", pp. 416-17, London, 1871)

The greatest of the Egyptian gods was Osiris. He was the father of the virgin-born savior, Horus, and was born of a virgin himself. Every year at Abydos the ancient Egyptians staged a mystery-play, a religious drama corresponding to the Catholic passion-

[2]

play. In this ritual were celebrated the sufferings, death and resurrection of Osiris. The kings of Egypt were ex-officio heads of the state religion. The Pharaoh, as a religious officer bore the title "His Holiness", the very title now addressed to the Roman Pope. But the Pharoah was not only the chief priest, he was considered a god incarnate. King Amenhotep III, of the 17th dynasty was represented as the son of the virgin Mutemua. The story of his miraculous birth was pictured on the inner walls of the Holy of Holies in the Temple of Luxor. "In this picture" asserts Samuel Sharpe, the Egyptologist, "we have the Annunciation, the Conception, the Birth and the Adoration, as described in the first and second chapters of Luke's gospel; and as we have historical assurance that the chapters in Matthew's gospel which contain the miraculous birth of Christ are an after addition not in the earliest manuscripts, it seems probable that these two poetical chapters in Luke may also be unhistorical, and borrowed from the Egyptian accounts of the miraculous birth of their kings." ("Egyptian Mythology and Egyptian Christianity", London, 1863; 2nd Edition, 1896). The early Christians had no trouble in spreading their doctrine in Egypt, for the old religion and the new were almost identical. "The knowledge of the ancient Egyptian religion which we now possess",—states the late Sir Wallis Budge in the preface to his work, "The Gods of the Egyptians"—, "fully justifies the assertion that the rapid growth and progress of Christianity in Egypt were due mainly to the fact that the new religion, which was preached there by St. Mark and his immediate followers, in all its essentials so closely resembled that which was the outcome of Osiris, Isis and Horus that popular opposition was entirely disarmed."

Another great pagan Christ was Krishna of India. The life of Krishna and the life of Jesus as recorded in the New Testament and New Testament Apocrypha are almost identical. We shall consider a few of the remarkable analogies in the biographies of these illustrious messiahs. (1) Krishna was born of the virgin Devaki, who was selected as the mother of the heavenly child on account of her purity.

Jesus was similarly born of a chaste virgin named Mary. (2) The birth of Krishna was announced by the appearance of his star in the firmament. The birth of Jesus was announced by the shining of his star in the sky. (See Matthew, II, 2).

(3) The Hindu Christ was of royal lineage, but was born in the most humble of surroundings, having first seen the light of day in a cave.

The Christian Christ, according to the apocryphal Gospel "Protevangelion", (a work attributed to James, the brother of Jesus), was born in a cave also. Canon Farrar in his famous "Life of Christ", states: "That the actual place of Christ's birth was a cave, is a very ancient tradition, and this cave used to be shown as the scene of the event even so early as the time of Justin Martyr (A. D. 150)." The grotto of the manger in the Church of the Nativity at Bethlehem, celebrated to this day as the birthplace of Jesus, is a cave. There in the rock may be seen a silver star inscribed in Latin as follows: "Hic de Virgine Maria Jesus Christus natus est".

(4) At the time of Krishna's birth the cave was illuminated by a mysterious light.

At the time of the birth of Jesus, "there was a great light in the cave, so that the eyes of Joseph and the midwife could not bear it". (New Testament Apocrypha, Protevangelion).

(5) Soon after birth the infant Krishna spoke to his mother. "Jesus spake even when he was in his cradle, and said to his mother: "Mary, I am Jesus the Son of God, that Word which thou didst bring forth according to the declaration of the Angel Gabriel unto thee, and my Father hath sent me for the salvation of th world." ("Gospel of the Infancy", New Testament Apocrypha).

(6) Krishna was born while his foster-father Nanda was away from home; being in the city to pay his tax to the king.

The birth of Jesus took place while his foster-father Joseph was in the city to pay his tax to the governor. (New Testament, Gospel according to Luke).

(7) As an infant, Krishna was recognized and adored by cowherds, who bowed down before him.

The infant Jesus was recognized and adored by shepherds, who prostrated themselves before him.

(8) The ruler of the country in which the Indian Christ was born, was the tyrant King Kansa. He sought the life of the holy child by ordering the massacre of all male children born during the night of Krishna's birth.

King Herod, as we read in the Bible, ordered the slaughter of the innocents, hoping to bring death to the Christ-child (Matthew, 2nd chapter).

(9) Nanda was warned by a heavenly voice to take the infant Krishna and flee across the Jumna River to Gakul, to escape from King Kansa.

Joseph was warned by a heavenly voice in a dream to "take the young child and his mother, and flee into Egypt," in order to escape the wrath of King Herod.

(10) In the city of Mathura (pronounced Mattra), Krishna performed many miracles.

While in Egypt, Jesus lived in a town named Matarea, and there performed many miracles. (N. T., Apocrypha).

(11) Krishna was crucified. In Indian art he is pictured as hanging on a cross with arms extended.

Jesus was crucified. In Christian art he is shown hanging on the cross, with arms extended.

(12) While on the cross, Krishna was pierced by an arrow.

While on the cross Jesus was pierced by a spear.

(13) Krishna said to the hunter who shot him: "Go, hunter, through my favor, to heaven, the abode of the gods".

Jesus said to one of the thieves: "Verily I say unto thee, this day shalt thou be with me in paradise." (Luke, XXIII, 43).

(14) When Krishna died, the light of the sun was blotted out at noon-day.

On the day of the death of Jesus Christ, the sun was darkened from the sixth to the ninth hour.

(15) Krishna descended into hell for the purpose of raising the dead, before returning to heaven.

Jesus Christ descended into hell to save the lost souls of the saints imprisoned there. According to orthodox creed, "He descended into hell, and on the third day he rose again from the dead." This descent into hell is discussed in detail in "The Gospel of Nicodemus", which is in the New Testament Apocrypha. In this gospel we read of Jesus descending to the infernal regions, a realm ruled over by Satan and his assistant the Prince of Hell. While the two rulers of hades are discussing ways and means of keeping the Christ out, his voice is heard, saying: "Lift up your gates, O ye Princes, and be ye lifted up O ye everlasting gates, and the King of Glory shall come in."

On hearing the voice, the Prince of Hell commanded his subordinates to: "Shut the brass gates, and make them fast with iron bars, and fight courageously". But this was of no avail, for the gates of hell prevailed not. The Christ appeared there in the form of a man, broke the fetters of the imprisoned saints and led them off to paradise.

(16) Krishna after his death and burial came back to life and arose from the grave.

The resurrection of Jesus from the tomb is familiar to all readers of the New Testament. (Matthew, XXVIII).

(17) Krishna ascended bodily into heaven, in the presence of a multitude of spectators.

So also did Jesus ascend to heaven in the flesh, the ascent being witnessed by many.

(18) In the sacred art of India, Krishna is always represented as a black man. The word "Krishna" literally means "the black".

In early Christian art, Jesus Christ is almost invariably shown with a black complexion.

(19) Krishna was the second person in the Hindu Trinity. This trinity consisted of Brahma, Vishnu and Siva. Krishna was Vishnu in human form.

The Christian Trinity consists of Father, Son and Holy Ghost. Jesus was the Son in human form.

(20) Krishna had a beloved disciple named Arjuna.

Similarly Jesus had a beloved disciple named John.

Another great Indian avatar was Buddha. The parallels between the lives of Christ Buddha and Christ Jesus are so striking, that certain Christians have accused the Hindus of borrowing from the Bible. We shall deal with a few of these analogies, but before doing so, it is necessary to say a few words about the life of Buddha. This great sage was born about 600 B. C., and bore the name of Prince Gautama. He was the son of King Suddhodana and Queen Maya. Though brought up in luxury, and wanting nothing, the prince became unhappy while still a young man. The problem of evil and the sufferings of the world weighed heavily upon his youthful conscience. He was overwhelmed with sorrow when he noticed:

"How lizard fed on ant, and snake on him,
And kite on both; and how the fish-hawk robbed
The fish-tiger of that which it had seized;
The shrike chasing the bulbul, which did hunt
The jewelled butterflies; till everywhere
Each slew a slayer, and in turn was slain,
Life living upon death. So the fair show,
Veiled one vast, grim, savage conspiracy
Of mutual murder, from the worm to man,
Who himself kills his fellow."

(From the poem, "The Light of Asia,"
by Sir Edwin Arnold).

So the young prince gave up his wealth, deserted his palace and wandered in the wilderness as a hermit. He suffered many hardships, but in his heart there was no rest. But one night in the forest he rested under the foliage of a gigantic tree. This tree became known as the famous "Bo-tree" (the tree of awakening) for here Prince Gautama became the "Buddha" (the Enlightened One). While sunk in profound meditation under the branches of the sacred tree, the sage found answers to those great questions which had so long agitated his mind. This life is not the only one, concluded he. Every man lives hundreds of lives. The good man strives to make each life better than the last. As he climbs higher on the ladder of life, sorrow and pain become less and less. Finally when selfishness and greed have been eliminated from the soul, the individual desires nothing, not even life. He attains "Nirvana", a dreamless delightful never-ending sleep. In the words of Sir Edwin Arnold:

"The aching craze to live ends, and life glides—
Lifeless—to nameless quiet, nameless joy,
Blessed Nirvana—sinless, stirless rest."

If we study the traditions, myths and legends of the life of Buddha, we are struck with the close resemblances they bear to the Biblical accounts of the life of Jesus Christ. Let us make a few comparisons.

(1) Buddha was born of the Virgin Maya or Mary.

Jesus was born of the Virgin Mary.

(2) Buddha's birthday was celebrated on December 25th.

Christmas, which falls on December 25th, is celebrated as the birthday of Jesus.

(3) The child Buddha was visited by wise men who recognized his divinity.

Likewise, the Christ-child was visited by wise men who adored him.

(4) Buddha was a dangerous child. King Bimbasara sought his life, fearing that if the child lived, his throne would be in danger.

King Herod, for the same reason, sought the life of the infant Jesus.

(5) When only twelve years old Buddha excelled the learned men of the temple in knowledge and wisdom.

The child Jesus confounded the doctors and elders in the temple, when only twelve years of age.

(6) The ancestry of Buddha is traced from his father Suddhodana, through various individuals back to Maha Sammata, the first monarch of the world.

The ancestry of Jesus is traced from his father Joseph, through various individuals back to Adam, the first man in the world.

(7) Buddha was tempted by Mara (the Author of Evil), who said to him: "Go not forth to adopt a religious life, and in seven days thou shalt become an emperor of the world." And Buddha answered: "Get thee away from me."

[5]

Jesus was tempted by Satan. The devil promised Jesus all the kingdoms of the world if he would fall down and worship him. But Jesus replied: "Get thee behind me Satan."

(8) The transfiguration of Buddha took place on a mountain top. A halo of bright light illluminated his person.

Jesus was transfigured on a mountain top; "and his face did shine as the sun, and his raiment as white as the light." Matthew, XVII, 1-2).

(9) After his earthly pilgrimage had been completed, Buddha ascended bodily to the celestial realms.

On the completion of his earthly mission, Jesus ascended in the flesh to paradise.

(10) Buddha is reputed to have said: "Let all the sins that were committed in this world fall on me, that the world may be delivered." (Quoted by Professor Max Muller in his "History of Ancient Sanscrit Literature").

Jesus is represented as delivering the world from sin, according to Christian dogma.

It is not necessary to present more parallels between the biographies of Jesus and Buddha, the above being quite enough for a short essay such as this. Students who are interested in a detailed study of the subject, are advised to consult the appropriate works which are listed in the bibliography. We shall treat some of the other pagan Christs very briefly, for to do otherwise would be only a repetition of what has already been said.

The religion of Mithra, originated in Persia, but in its latter days overspread the Roman Empire; being a powerful rival of early Christianity. In this religion, God is considered too spiritual to have any contact with the world. So the Infinite manifested himself in the person of Mithra, who is mediator between God and man. It is recorded that Mithra was born of a Virgin, on the 25th of December. The place of birth was a cave. His earliest worshippers were shepherds. He was accompanied by twelve companions. Mithraists kept the Sabbath day holy, and celebrated the Eucharist by eating wafers embellished with a cross.

The greast festivals of the Mithraic religion were those of the Birth, which fell on Christmas, and of the Resurrection, which fell on Easter.

Bacchus of Greece was one worshipped as a savior. He was also virgin-born on December 25th. His sacred emblem was the letters IHS, now seen in Christian churches.

Quetzalcoatl was a virgin-born savior of ancient Mexico. He was tempted and fasted for forty days. He is shown in paintings in the Borgian MS., hanging on a cross. Impressions of nails are seen on the hands and feet. He died upon the cross as an atonement for the sins of man. He is pictured as a man of black complexion. After his crucifixion he rose from the dead and went into the East. The devotees of Quetzalcoatl were expecting his second coming when the Spaniards under Cortez invaded the country early in the 16th Century.

Adonis or Tammuz of Babylonia, was believed to have been born of a virgin, to have died a cruel death and descended into hell, to have arisen from the tomb and ascended to heaven. In midsummer his worshippers wept over an effigy of his dead body, which was washed with water, anointed with oil and clothed in a red robe, amid clouds of incense. On the next day was celebrated his resurrection, with the worshippers shouting "The Lord is risen." Finally, his ascension in the presence of his devotees was enacted as the conclusion of the festival.

Attis of Phrygia was said to have been the son of the Virgin Nana, and he was known as the Good Shepherd. In his prime he mutilated himself and bled to death under a sacred pine-tree. In ancient Rome the festival of his death and resurrection was celebrated from March 22nd to March 25th. On March 22nd a pine-tree was cut and an effigy of the dead god was tied to the trunk. Attis was thus shown as "slain and hanged on a tree." (See New Testament, Acts V., 30). The effigy was afterwards buried in a tomb. On the night of the 24th of March, the priests visited the tomb and found it empty, the god having risen from the dead on the third day. On the 25th the resurrection was celebrated with great joy; a sacramental meal being partaken of, and devotees of the deity were baptized with blood, which was supposed to wash away their sins. They were then said to have been "born again."

Thus far our discussion of pagan and Christian parallels have been mainly by way of comparison and contrast. Our next task will be chiefly one of analysis; a consideration of the origin and meaning of these ancient beliefs. Scholars recognize two types of savior-gods, namely: (1) Vegetation-gods and (2) Sun-gods. The close resemblances between the stories told of these divinities and those related of the Christian Savior in the Gospels have caused many students of hierology (the science of religion), to doubt the historicity of Jesus. They regard him as a mythical character, a personification of the Spirit of Vegetation or an incarnation of the Sun, or most probably a blend of both. The most eminent representatives of this school, living and dead, are Charles F. Dupuis, Constantine Francis Count de Volney, Professor P. L. Couchoud, Professor William Benjamin Smith, L. Gordon Rylands, Rev. Robert Taylor, Rev. Richard B. Westbrook, Bishop Wm. Montgomery Brown, Gerald Massey, the Rt. Hon. John M. Robertson and Prof. Arthur Drews. The mythicists, as they are called, have defended their position with a great deal of skill and ability. This ultra-rationalistic position was opposed by Sir James George Frazer, Professor Joseph McCabe and the late Sir Arthur Weigall. They claim that even though the Gospel narrative be reduced to a tissue of myths and legends, it is still possible to consider Jesus as an historical figure. After being deified, these traditions could easily have been woven into the story of his life. Whether the vegetation cults or the solar cults affected Christianity the most, we do not pretend to say, but we shall discuss both theories, and the reader will no doubt compare their merits and reach his own conclusion. The great authorities on myths and rites of vegetation, are Sir J. G. Frazer and Grant Allen. The gist of the vegetation-myth theory, however, is brilliantly stated by an eminent psychiatrist, as follows:

"Many gods besides Christ have been supposed to die, be resurrected and ascend to heaven. This idea has now been traced back to its origin among primitive people in the annual death and resurrection of crops and plant life generally. This explains the world-wide prevalence of the notion. Among still more primitive tribes, as Grant Allen showed, it is not yet understood that sown corn sprouts because of the spring sunshine, and they attribute the result to divine agency. To this end they are accustomed at seed-time to kill their tribal good—either in human or animal form—and scatter the flesh and blood over the sown fields. They believe that the seeds will not grow unless the god is sacrificed and added to them in this manner. When, therefore, the crop appears, they never doubt that it is their god coming to life again. It is from this erroneous belief of primitive tribes that Christianity today derives its belief in Christ's Death and Resurrection." ("Psychology and Religion", p. 97, by Dr. David Forsyth, London 1935).

The chief writers on the astronomical elements of natural theology, are Massey, Doane, Volney, Dupuis, Higgins, Carpenter and Robertson. The father of the solar-myth theory was the French savant Charles Francois Dupuis. In the fourth centry the Roman scholar Macrobius had promulgated the theory that the various pagan gods were symbolizations of the sun, but it was left for Dupuis in the latter part of the 18th Century to place the theory on a scientific foundation. The high points of this hypothesis are summarized in the following extract from the American edition of Dupuis' celebrated work, "The Origin of all Religious Worship":

"The god is born about December 25th, without sexual intercourse, for the Sun, entering the winter solstice, emerges in the sign of Virgo, the heavenly virgin. His mother remains ever-virgin, since the rays of the Sun, passing through the zodiacal sign, leave it intact. His infancy is begirt by dangers, because the new-born Sun is feeble in the midst of winter's fogs and mists, which threaten to devour him; his life is one of toil and peril, culminating at the spring equinox in a final struggle with the powers of darkness. At that period the day and night are equal, and both fight for the mastery. Though the night veil the Sun and he seems dead; though he has descended cut of sight, below the earth, yet he rises again triumphant, and he rises in the sign of the Lamb (the constellation Aries), and is thus the Lamb of God, carrying away the darkness and death of the winter months. Henceforth he triumphs, growing ever stronger and more brilliant. He ascends into the zenith, and there he glows, on the right hand of God, himself God, the very substance of the Father, the brightness of his glory, and the express image of his person, upholding all things by his life-giving power."

Vegetation cults, we have good reason to believe, are far more ancient than stellar or solar cults, so we shall devote a little space to a discussion of vegetation rites before proceeding with our consideration of astro-theological doctrine. Many ancient peoples annually held a vegetation-god sacrifice. Originally, the victim sacrificed to the god was the king. The king represented the god in human form, and was threfore considered divine. It was believed that the prosperity of the tribe or nation depended on the physical well being of the ruler. If the king should become old and feeble, it was believed the country would suffer a similar decline. So by killing the monarch in his prime, and replacing him with younger blood the prosperity of the realm was preserved. Kings got tired of being killed of course, so in due time, the king's son was substituted for the divine father, and was therefore known as the son of the god. The son was given royal honors for a period, and then sacrificed. He was generally slain while bound to a sacred tree, often with arms outstretched in the form of a cross. The resurrection of the murdered victim was believed to occur after a time—a three day period being the most popular — the resurrection representing the return of vegetation. As men became more civilized, a condemned criminal was substituted. And as a rule his limbs were broken while he hung on the sacrificial tree or cross. The book of Esther, in the Bible seems to have been based on one of these primitive sacrificial rites.

"Such a drama, if we are right," declares Sir J. G. Frazer, "was the original story of Esther, and Mordecai, or (to give their older names) Ishtar and Marduk. It was played in Babylonia, and from Babylonia the returning captives brought it to Judea, where it was acted, rather as an historical than a mythical piece, by players who, having to die in grim earnest on a cross or gallows, were naturally drawn from the gaol rather than the green-room. A chain of causes, which, because we cannot follow them might in the loose language of common life, be called an accident, determined that the part of the dying god in this annual play should be thrust upon Jesus of Nazareth, whom the enemies he had made in high places by his outspoken strictures were resolved to put out of the way." ("The Golden Bough", Vol. IX, "The Scapegoat", p. 400). The book of Esther is, therefore non-historical, Esther being the Semite goddess, Ishtar; Mordecai, the Babylonian god, Marduk, and Haman, a god of the Elamites. The romance is probably based on the Babylonian festival of the Sacaea. This ceremony, we learn from the Chaldean historian, Berosus, was celebrated annually in ancient Babylon. During the celebration which lasted five days, masters and servants changed places, the servants giving orders and the masters obeying them. A prisoner, under sentence of death, was dressed in the robes of the king, and placed on the regal throne. This mock king, who bore the title of Zoganes, issued whatever commands he pleased, ate and drank all he desired, and was allowed to enjoy the society of the king's concubines. But after the five days were up, he was bereft of his regal robes, scourged and then either hanged or crucified.

Among the ancient Hebrews there was celebrated a similar rite, known as the Bar-abbas sacrifice. At the time of the passover, a condemned criminal was turned into a mock king, and called Bar-Abbas (Son of the Father). It seems that he was finally crucified. According to the Gospel narrative, Jesus appears to have been slain as a substitute for the Bar-Abbas victim. His enemies are shown requesting Filate to let the condemned criminal go free, so that they might put Jesus in his place. "The victms of these human sacrifices were generally crucified", asserts Sir Arthur Weigall, "or else killed and then 'hung on a tree' until the evening.

In this regard it is interesting to notice that in the Acts the writer mistakenly speaks of Jesus as having been slain and then hanged on a tree, as though this were a common phrase coming readily to his mind; and the word 'hanged' is frequently used in Greek to denote crucifixion." ("The Paganism in our Christianity", pp. 77-78, N. Y. & London, 1928).

It is now advisable to return to our discussion of the astronomical elements in the ancient creeds. Dupuis, after much careful research, was convinced that the Christian savior was a mythical character and the story of his life was nothing more than the story of the sun (of which he was a personification), as it made its annual journey through the twelve signs of the zodiac. The zodiac is an imaginary band encircling the celestial sphere. It stretches eight degrees on each side of the Ecliptic (the apparent path of the sun). The zodiac is divided into twelve equal divisions, each one corresponding to one month. Due to the annual revolution of the earth, the sun appears to make one complete circuit through the zodiac in one year, staying in each sign one month. The signs of the zodiac and the constellations of the zodiac were originally the same, but due to the procession of the equinoxes, each sign moves westward into the next constellation in about 2155 years. A sign therefore makes a complete circuit of the heavens in about 26,000 years. According to Professor Harding, the well known astronomer and mathematician, the signs and constellations of the zodiac coincided about 300 B. C., and before that about 26,000 B. C.

Since they were widely known thousands of years before 300 B.C., then they evidently originated not later than about 26,000 B.C. (The reader who has difficulty in following this astronomical data, should obtain a popular book on astronomy, such as, "Astronomy: The Splendor of the Heavens brought down to Earth", by Professor Arthur M. Harding, and should read especially chapter VI, which is entitled, "the Story of the Stars." If the reader happens to be in New York, he should also visit the Hayden Planetarium, which is a part of the great American Museum of Natural History). The constellations of the zodiac have the following names: Aries (the Ram or Lamb), Taurus (the Bull or Ox), Gemini (the Twins), Cancer (the Crab), Leo (the Lion), Virgo (the Virgin), Libra (the Balance), Scorpio (the Scorpion), Sagittarius (the Archer), Capricornus (the Goat), Aquarius (the Water-carrier), Pisces (the Fishes). The following speculations on the origin of the names of the constellations are about as accurate as any list that might be compiled, the majority of students of the subject being in general agreement upon them. The constellations of the Lamb, the Ox and the Twins, were star-groups thru which the sun passed in the spring; in which time of the year occurred the seasons of sheep-raising, ploughing and goat-breeding. The Twins were originally the two kids, since the young of goats are frequently born two at a time. The stars of the Crab were so called, because the sun reached its most northern point in that constellation, and then returned towards the south, figuratively moving backwards like a crab. The Lion is that star-group thru which the sun moved in July, when its heat was most powerful, being compared with the most ferocious of the animals. The Virgin, is an emblem of the harvest season, when the young girls were sent out to glean in the fields. The Balance is the constellation in which the sun moved when day and night were equal in length, just as if they were weighed in a balance. The stars of the Scorpion were hidden by the sun during the season of unhealthy weather, and of plagues, which were imagined to strike like a scorpion. Stars called the Archer, reigned over the hunting season, when the hunter shot game with the bow and arrow. In the Goat, the sun reached the lowest point in its course, after which it began to climb towards the north again, just as the wild goat climbs towards the summit of the hill. The Water-carrier marked the position of the solar orb during the rainy season. The stars of the Fishes, constituted that group through which the sun passed when the fishing season was at its height.

The Bible is rich in astronomical symbolism. We read in the Apocalypse: "And round about the throne, were four beasts full of eyes before and behind. And the first beast was like a lion, and the second beast

[9]

like a calf, and the third beast had a face as a man , and the fourth beast was like a flying eagle." (Revelation: IV, 6-7). The eyes of the beasts are the stars, and the creatures themselves are the constellations which 5,000 years ago were situated at the cardinal points of the celestial sphere. Each star-group was marked by one conspicuously bright star, and said constellations were located as follows: Taurus (the Bull), at the vernal Equinox; Aquila (the Eagle), at the Autumnal Equinox; Leo (the Lion), at the Summer Solstice; and Aquarius (the man), at the Winter Solstice. The presence of astronomical myth-motives in the New Testament are graphically pointed out by Rev. Westbrook, who states that:

"Jesus is represented as having been born in a cave or stable at the moment of midnight. At that period the constellation Virgo is cut exactly in half by the eastern horizon, the sun itself being beneath in the zodiacal sign of Capricorn, which was also called the 'Stable of Augeas' that Hercules was set to cleanse. Justin Martyr corroborates this by stating that Christ was born when the sun (Mithra) takes his birth in the stable of Augeas, coming as a second Hercules to cleanse a foul world . . . ."Astrological correspondences are carefully maintained all through the gospel narrative. The apostles represent the twelve months, each of them being sent or commissioned to announce him (the sun) to the people. The special events and their dates are commemorated by the Church so as to be coincident with astrological data. The designation 'Lamb of God' comes directly from the fact that the crucifixion was placed at the time the sun crosses the equinoctial line in March, and so entered the zodiacal sign of Aries, the Lamb. He was thus 'slain before the foundation of the world', or year, and takes away the sins or evils of winter. Having descended into hell, or the winter period, he rises from the dead. He is now enthroned; the four beasts, denoting the four chief constellations in each quarter of the zodiacal circle—Taurus, Leo, Aquila and Aquarius—adore him, and the twenty-four elders (or hours) fall down and worship him. The miracle of turning water into wine is done every year, as Addison has sung:

'May the sun refine
The grape's soft juice and mellow it to wine.'

"The curse of the fig-tree is visited on every plant that is feeble and poorly rooted when the suns heat comes upon it. John the Baptist says of Jesus: 'He must increase, but I must decrease'. The 24th of June, St. John's day, is the last of the summer solstice, from which period the days shorten, as on the contrary, from the 25th of December, the natal day of Jesus, they lengthen. 'This is the sixth month with her that was called barren', said the angel Gabriel to Mary on the 25th of March, the Annunciation, nine months before Christmas. On the 5th of August the Church celebrates the Assumption of the Blessed Virgin into the heavenly chamber of the King of Kings, and accordingly the constellation Virgo also disappears, being eclipsed by the light and glory of the sun... Three weeks later the sun has moved on in the sky, permitting the constellation again to appear; and accordingly the Church celebrates the 8th of September as the anniversary of the nativity of the Blessed Virgin.

"The prominent pagan symbols which are now adopted by the Christian prelacy are generally astronomical. Astrology and religion always went hand in hand, and have not been legally divorced. At an earlier period the sun entered the zodiacal sign of Taurus at the vernal equinox. This fact led to the adoption of the bull or calf as a symbol of the Deity. We notice this fact all over the ancient world, and in some modern peoples that have not had a learned caste of priests. Every 2152 years the zodiac shifts back one sign-i.e. one-twelfth of its whole extent. Hence, eventually, Aries, the Ram or Lamb, took the place of the Bull to represent the god of spring. The paschal lamb, the ram-headed god Amen of Egypt, and the lamb of Christian symbolism thus came into existence. Since that the constellation Pisces has become the equinoctial sign, and the Fish is the symbol of the Church. Hence the bishop of Rome employs the seal of the fisherman, and the Gospel narrative has made St. Peter a 'fisher'. In this way the entire passion of Jesus from the crucifixion to the ascension is astronomic". ("The Eliminator: or Skeleton Keys to Sacerdotal Secrets", pp. 245-250, by Richard B. Westbrook, D. D., Philadelphia, 1892).

In the study of comparative religion the student notices that many of the ancient savior-gods were said to appear on earth at definite intervals of time. The most common period was in round numbers, six-hundred years. For instance, Gautama Buddha was said to have been born about 600 B. C., while Krishna is supposed to have lived about 1200 B.C. The sacred monogram of Christ, the letters IHS, so frequently seen in Christian churches, is connected with this 600 year cycle in a most interesting manner. This fact is instructively recorded by Dr. Westbrook, as follows:

"The church interprets these letters to stand for Jesus, Salvator Hominem—i. e., Jesus the savior of men. The initiates read them as numerals which stand for 608; which is the exact period of a solar-lunar cycle—i.e., the number of years which pass before the sun and moon occupy the same relative positions in the heavens. According to the astral theology of ancient religious systems, this cycle of 608 (or 600) years represented a messianic period, at the completion of which a new messiah or avatar or savior was born upon the earth." ("Eliminator", p. 298).

This cycle of 600 or 608 years appears mysterious unless we study it closely. For example, it was very anciently known that the solar and lunar calendars coincided every eight years, when the full moon falls on either the shortest or longest day of the year. This octennial cycle, when multiplied by 75, gives us 600. When 8 is multiplied by 76, we get 608 as a result. So we see that the messianic cycle is simply a multiple of the eight year cycle. This 600 year cycle was known among the ancient Babylonians as the Neros.

The letters IHS present an absorbing problem. These letters were the sacred monogram of the Greek god Dionysus or Bacchus. The Christians adopted them, as they did many other symbols, from the pagan. These letters form the root of the name Jesus. IHS when translated from Greek to Latin becomes IES. Adding the Latin masculine suffix—US, we get IES plus US, which equals IESUS. In English the I becomes J, hence we get JESUS.

The Christian monogram Chi-rho is also of pagan origin. The emblem is so called, because it is composed of the Greek letters X (chi) and P (rho). It was originally sacred to the Egyptian sun-god, Horus, according to that veteran Egyptologist, Sir Flinders Petrie. It is claimed by Sir Godfrey Higgins in his "Anacalypsis", that: "These two letters in the old Samaritan, as found on coins, stand, the first for 400, the second for 200 $=$ 600." If this is so, then the symbols IHS and Chi-rho appear to be closely related.

Christianity in its infancy was an oriental religion, and since astral theology is a fundamental element in the oriental cults, Christianity therefore was profoundly influenced by it. The universality of star and sun worship, among the ancients, is beautifully revealed in the inimitable poetic prose of Volney:

"Ye inhabitants of India, in vain you cover yourselves with the veil of mystery: the hawk of your god Vishnu is but one of the thousand emblems of the sun in Egypt; and your incarnations of a god in the fish, the boar, the lion, the tortoise, and all his monstrous adventures, are ony the metamorphoses of the sun, who, passing through the signs of the twelve animals (or the zodiac), was supposed to assume their figures, and perform their astronomical functions. People of Japan, your bull, which breaks the mundane egg, is only the bull of the zodiac, which in former times opened the seasons, the age of creation, the vernal equinox. It is the same bull Apis which Egypt adored, and which your ancestors, Jewish Rabbins, worshipped in the golden calf. This is still your bull, followers of Zoroaster, which sacrificed in the symbolic mysteries of Mithra, poured out his blood which fertilized the earth. And ye Christians, your bull of the Apocalypse, with his wings, symbol of the air, has no other origin; and your lamb of God, sacrificed, like the bull of Mithra, for the salvation of the world, is only the same sun, in the sign of the celestial ram, whicn, in a later age, opening the equinox in his turn, was supposed to deliver the world from evil, that is to say, from the constellation of the serpent, from that great snake, the parent of winter, the emblem of the Ahriman or Satan of the Persians, your school masters. Yes, in vain does your imprudent zeal consign idolators to the torments of the Tartarus which they invented; the whole basis of your system is only the worship of the sun, with whose attributes you have decorated your principal personage. It is the sun which, under the name of Horus, was born, like your God, at the winter solstice, in the arms of the celestial virgin, and who passed a childhood of obscurity. It is he that, under the name of Osiris, persecuted by Typhon and by the tyrants of the air, was put to death, shut up in a dark tomb, emblem of the hemisphere of winter, and afterwards, ascending from the inferior zone towards the zenith of heaven, arose again from the dead, triumphant over the giants and the angels of destruction." (Volney's "Ruins of Empires", pp. 124-125, New York, 1926).

The solar myth theory does not have the same vogue today, that it had in the 19th century, but it is still of great importance as a partial explanation of the Christ-myth. This is shown very clearly by the Rt. Hon. J. M. Robertson in his "Christianity and Mythology" and "Pagan Christs", and by L. Gordon Rylands in his work, "Did Jesus Ever Live?" Mr. Rylands points out that Jesus is a Greek name, of which the Hebrew equivalent is Joshua. The worshippers of Joshua seem to have enacted a yearly mystery-drama in which a representative of the divine Joshua was slain. These rites were practiced in secret while the priests of Jehovah were in power, but came into the light again after the fall of Jerusalem, since after that event, secrecy was no longer necessary. According to this theory, as explained by Mr. Rylands, Jesus was not an historic personage, but a character in a drama, just as Hamlet and Othello are characters in the plays of Shakespeare. "What is clear", declares Mr. Robertson, "is that the central narrative of the gospel biography, the story of the Last Supper, the Agony, Betrayal, Trial and Crucifixion, is neither a contemporary report nor a historical tradition, but the simple transcript of a Mystery-Drama." ("A Short History of Christianity", p. 9, J. M. Robertson, London 1931).

To those unacquainted with historical criticism, especially the historical criticism of the Bible, the theories here outlined will seem fantastic. Traditional views on the Bible and on the origins of Christianity, have been shown by modern scholarship to be quite untenable. The average layman is familiar only with the King James' version of the Bible. This particular English translation of the Bible dates back to 1611 A. C. a little over 300 years ago. There have been other English translations since that date, but as a rule, only scholars are familiar with them. The layman generally does not know that the Bible is not one book, but a whole library of books, of which the authorized version is only a small part. For instance, "The Book of Enoch" is found only in the Ethiopian version of The Bible. Popular ideas on the antiquity and accuracy of Biblical texts are quite erroneous. The oldest parts of the Old Testament date from about the 12th Century B. C. This is the opinion of the experts, but they freely admit that the oldest Hebrew Old Testament MS., dates back only to the 10th Century of the Christian Era. Compare this with "The Book of the Dead", the Bible of the Egyptians, which dates back to about 4,000 B. C. There are no contemporary documents dealing with the life of Jesus either in sacred or profane history. Our chief sources of information are the genuine Pauline Epistles, which were written from about 52 to 64 A. D., and the four Gospels. The dates of the writing of the Gospels, according to the best authorities, are as follows: Mark 70 to 100 A. D.); Luke (about 100 A. D.); Matthew (100 to 110 A. D.); John (some time between 100 and 160 A. D.). The oldest Greek New Testament manuscript dates from the 4th Centry A. D. (This is the famous "Codex Sinaiticus", now in the British Museum, in London).

One of the best of the recent books dealing with the life and teachings of Jesus is Robert Keable's work, entitled "The Great Galilean." Mr. Keable gives the following instructive summary of what is actually known concerning the man Jesus:

"No man knows sufficient of the early life of Jesus to write a biography of him. For that matter, no one knows enough for the normal "Times" obituary notice of a great man. If regard were had to what we should call, in correct speech, definitely historical facts, scarcely three lines could be filled.

"Moreover, if newspapers had been in existence, and if that obituary notice had had to be written in the year of his death, no editor could have found in the literature of his day so much as his name. Yet few periods of the ancient world were so well documented as the period of Augustus and Tiberius. But no contemporary knew of his existence. Even a generation later, a spurious passage in Josephus, a questionable reference in Suetonius, and the mention of a name that may be his by Tacitus—that is all. His first mention in any surviving document, secular or religious, is twenty years after." (Quoted by Dr. Harry Elmer Barnes, in his "Twilight of Christianity," p. 402, New York, 1931).

December the 25th, is celebrated as the birthday of Jesus, but no authority believes that it is the correct day. In fact, up to the 4th Century, the birthday of the Christ was celebrated on the 6th of January. Why the date was changed to December 25th, is explained to us by an ancient Christian Syrian writer, who says that:

"The reason why the fathers transferred the celebration of the sixth of January to the twenty-fifth of December was this. It was a custom of the heathen to celebrate on the same twenty-fifth of December the birthday of the Sun, at which they kindled lights in token of festivity. In these solemnities and festivities the Christians also took part. Accordingly when the doctors of the Church perceived that the Christians had a leaning to this festival, they took counsel and resolved that the true Nativity should be solemnized on that day and the festival of the Epiphany on the sixth of January. Accordingly, along with this custom, the practice has prevailed of kindling fires till the sixth".

The year of the birth of Jesus is generally given as 4 B. C., but this is by no means certain. The Gospel according to Matthew declares that he was born when Herod was King of Judea. The Gospel according to Luke states that his birth occurred when Cyrenius (or Quirinius) was Governor of Syria. There is here a discrepancy of at least ten years, since Herod died in 4 B. C., while Cyrenius did not become Governor of Syria until 7 A. D.

As to Easter, the very name shows its pagan origin, the festival being named after the Norse goddess Oestra or Eastre. Easter Sunday is the first Sunday after the first full moon after the beginning of Spring. Since the vernal Equinox falls on March 21st, Easter may be celebrated as early as March 22nd, or as late as April 25th. The early Christians, in Italy, Gaul (France) and Phrygia celebrated the Resurrection on the 25th of March. This date was evidently adopted from the Attis cult. So we see that both Christmas and Easter are of pagan origin.

There is a very strange omission in the Gospel biographies of Jesus. We see the boy Christ, at the age of twelve confounding the learned doctors in the Temple. We hear no more of him until he reaches the age of thirty. Why this gap of 18 years? There is a speculation that Jesus travelled in the Far East and studied at the feet of the wise men of India, during the interim, but this is only a fancy. The only plausible explanation known to the author of this exposition, is the one given by the English Egyptologist, Gerald Massey. The following extract is from Massey's lecture on "The Historical Jesus and Mythical Christ":

" In Egypt the year began soon after the Summer Solstice, when the sun descended from its mid-summer height, lost its force and lessened in its size. This represented Osiris, who was born of the virgin Mother as the child Horus, the diminished infantile sun of Autumn; the suffering, wounded, bleeding Messiah, as he was represented. He descended into hell, or hades, where he was transformed into the virile Horus, and rose again as the sun of the resurrection at Easter. In these two characters of Horus on the two horizons, Osiris furnished the dual type for the Canonical Christ .. The first was the child Horus, who always remained a child. In Egypt the boy or girl wore the Horus-lock of childhood until 12 years of age. Thus childhood ended about the twelfth year. But although adultship was then entered upon by the youth, and transformation of the boy into manhood began, the full adultship was not attained until 30 years of age . . . . As with the man, so it is with the God; and the second Horus, the same God in his second character, is the Khemt or Khem-Horus, the typical adult of 30 years. The God up to twelve years was Horus, the child of Isis, the mother's child, the weakling. The virile Horus (the sun in its vernal strength), the adult of 30 years, was representative of the Fatherhood, and this Horus is the anointed son of Osiris. These two characters of Horus the child, and Horus the adult of 30 years, are reproduced in the only two phases of the life of Jesus in the Gospels. John furnishes no historic dates for the time when the Word was incarnated and became flesh; nor for the childhood of Jesus; nor for the transformation into the Messiah. But Luke tells us that the child of twelve years was the wonderful youth, and that he increased in wisdom and stature. This is the length of years assigned to Horus the child; and this phase of the child-Christ's life is followed by the baptism and anointing, the descent of the pubescent spirit with the consecration of the Messiah in Jordan, when Jesus 'began to be about 30 years of age' . . .And just as the second Horus was regenerated, and this time begotten of the father, so in the transformation scene of the baptism in Jordan, the father authenticates the change into full adultship, with the voice from heaven saying: 'This is my beloved son, in whom I am well pleased'; the spirit of pubescence, or the Ruach, being represented by the descending dove, called the spirit of God . . . .

"As the child-Horus, Osiris comes down to earth; he enters matter, and becomes mortal. He is born like the Logos, or 'as a Word'. His father is Seb, the earth, whose consort is Nu, the heaven, one of whose names is Meri, the Lady of Heaven; and these two are the prototypes of Joseph and Mary. He is said to cross the earth a substitute, and to suffer vicariously as the Savior, Redeemer and Justifier of men. In these two characters there was constant conflict between Osiris and Typhon, the Evil Power, or Horus and Set, the Egyptian Satan. At the Autumn Equinox, the devil of darkness began to dominate; this was the Egyptian Ju-

das, who betrayed Osiris to death at the last supper. On the day of the Great Battle at the vernal Equinox, Osiris conquered as the ascending God, the Lord of the growing light. Both these struggles are portrayed in the Gospels. In the one Jesus is betrayed to his death by Judas; in the other he rises superior to Satan. The latter conflict followed immediately after the Baptism. In this way: when the sun was half way around, from the Lion sign, it crossed the river of the Waterman, the Egyptian Iarutana, Hebrew Jordan, Greek Eridanus. In this water the baptism occurred, and the transformation of the child-Horus into the virile adult, the conqueror of the evil power, took place. Horus becomes hawk-headed, just where the dove ascended and abode on Jesus. Both birds represented the virile soul that constituted the anointed one at puberty. By this added power, Horus vanquished Set, and Jesus overcame Satan." (Massey's principal works on Egypt are listed in the bibliography. They are unfortunately, out of print and difficult to obtain.)

Many incidents, of the Gospel stories can be explained only as myths. We read of Satan leading Jesus to the mountain top. The devil has been represented in Jewish and Christian folklore and art in the form of a goat. We see Satan in medieval paintings with the hooves, horns and tail of a goat. The Greek god Pan was part goat, and is represented as leading Zeus to the mountain-top. In ancient Bablyon the Goat was the emblem of the zodiacal sign, Capricorn. The sun reached the lowest point in the celestial sphere in this sign, after which it began to climb towards the highest point. So the goat-god is imagined to lead the sun-god toward the highest point, figuratively called the mountain top.

In Greek mythology we read of the savior Dionysus, on one occasion, riding upon two asses, which afterwards he had changed into celestial constellations. Jesus is pictured as riding into Jerusalem upon two asses, i. e. upon "an ass and colt, the foal of an ass." (Matthew, XXI, 5, 7).

In Babylonia, the symbol of the zodiacal sign of Cancer, in which the sun reaches the highest point of its path, was the Ass and Foal. Robertson, in his "Christianity and Mythology", tells of an ancient Gnostic gem, which has engraved upon it an ass and foal; and also a crab, which is the classic emblem of the zodiacal sign of Cancer. Besides these images the gem contains an abbreviated Latin inscription, which translated into English, reads as follows: "Our Lord Jesus Christ the Son of God." So we see that certain Gnostics recognized the astrological element in the Gospel narrative.

Many learned Christian scholars do not believe that Jesus had any idea of starting a new religion or establishing a Church. They believe that the real founder of institutional Christianity was St. Paul. Yet we read of Jesus referring to Peter as the rock upon which the Church is to be built. St. Peter is also popularly represented as the gate-keeper of heaven. The name Peter comes from the Greek word Petra, which means rock. This may be a pseudonym, since he is referred to also as Simon Peter. That is, he may have been named Simon, and was called "the Rock", because of some trait of character, just as General "Stonewall" Jackson was so called, because of the fact that he stood up against the enemy like a stone wall. It is interesting to note that there was a popular Semitic god named Simon, and that the ancient Egyptian god Petra, was represented as being the door-keeper of heaven, the earth and the underworld.

A large number of modern Christians do not accept the Gospel accounts of the Resurrection. They claim that they believe in a spiritual rather than a physical resurrection. This view is not as heretical as it might seem. According to Mosheim, the eminent authority on ecclesiastical history: "The prevalent opinion among early Christians was that Christ existed in appearance only." The orthodox Christian does not believe in the crucifixion and resurrection of Osiris, Krishna, Adonis or Attis, because, claims he there is no historical evidence to justify such belief. The impartial student of history might urge the same objections against Christian doctrine. Dean Milman in his scholarly "History of Latin Christianity," states that: "The Gnostic sects denied that Christ was born at all, or that he died." The Gnostics were eclectic religious philosophers. The name Gnostic is based on the Greek word gnosis, which means knowledge. The Gnostics, were those who knew, just as the modern Agnostics are those who do not know. The Gnostics, says the historian, Edward Gibbon, were "the most polite, the most learned, and the most wealthy of the Christian name." There were a number of Gnostic sects flourishing in the second century. These religious mystics claimed that they possessed certain secret teachings of Jesus which the Apostles had kept hidden from the common people. One of the chief Gnostic leaders was Basilides, who claimed to have received the esoteric doctrines of Jesus from St. Matthew. He taught that there were 365 heavens, each one created by a different generation of angels, who were descended from the unbegotten Father—God. The lowest of the numerous heavens is the Christian Paradise, ruled over by Jehovah, a minor god who has nothing to do with the higher heavens. Jesus, according to Basilides, was not the son of Jehovah, but of the Father-God, who did not permit his death on the cross, but substituted Simon the Cyrenian, who was crucified in his stead. Another Gnostic sect, the Mandeans, denied that Jesus was the Messiah, recognizing John the Baptist instead. A remnant of this sect is still extant, at present dwelling on the shores of the Persian Gulf.

There is an old legend of obscure origin, which states that Jesus did not die on the cross, but only fainted; and that he was afterwards revived and spirited away into the country. There he remained for a time in exile, until he finally met Paul. He accused Paul of teaching false doctrines in his name. A struggle is said to have ensued, in which Paul slew Jesus. Perhaps this part of the legend is only an allegory, symbolizing the diametrical opposition of the rival philsophies of Jesus and Paul.

The historical evidence of the darkness at the time of the Passion is considered by Edward Gibbon, who writes:

"But how shall we excuse the supine inattention of the Pagan and philosophic world to those evidences which were presented by the hand of Omnipotence, not to their reason, but to their senses? During the age of Christ, of His Apostles, and of their first disciples, the doctrine which they preached was confirmed by innumerable prodigies. The lame walked, the blind saw, the sick were healed, the dead were raised, demons were expelled, and the laws of Nature were frequently suspended for the benefit of the Church. But the sages of Greece and Rome turned aside from the awful spectacle, and pursuing the ordinary occupations of life and study, appeared unconscious of any alterations in the moral or physical government of the world. Under the sign of Tiberius the whole earth, or at least a celebrated province of the Roman Empire, was involved in a preternatural darkness of three hours. Even this miraculous event, which ought to have excited the wonder, the curiosity, and the devotion of all mankind, passed without notice in an age of science and history. It happened during the lifetime of Seneca and the elder Pliny, who must have experienced the immediate effects, or received the earliest intellignce of the prodigy. Each of these philosophers in a laborious work, has recorded all of the great phenomena of Nature, earthquakes, meteors, comets and eclipses, which his indefatigable curiosity could collect. Both the one and the other have omitted to mention the greatest phenomenon to which the mortal eye has been witness since the creation of the globe. A distinct chapter of Pliny is designed for eclipses of an extraordinary nature and unusual duration; but he contents himself with describing the singular defect of light which followed the murder of Caesar, when, during the greatest part of the year, the orb of the sun appeared pale and without splendor. This season of obscurity which cannot surely be compared with the preternatural darkness of the Passion, had been already celebrated by most of the poets and historians of that memorable age." (Gibbon's "History of the Decline and Fall of the Roman Empire" Chapter XV).

It is claimed by many devout Christians that the Golden Rule is the very essence of Christianity, and that this moral precept was not taught by any of the pre-christian religions. History does support this claim. The Golden Rule ("Do unto others as you would have them do unto you"), was taught by Confucious in China and by Buddha in India, more than 500 years before Christ. Seventy

years before Christ, Rabbi Hillel, president of the Sanhedrin of Jerusalem, expounded the Golden Rule to the Jews, in the following words:

"Do not to others what you would not have them do to you. This is the substance of the law."

The Lord's prayer is also of pre-Christian origin. It seems to be based on the Jewish Kadish prayer, which in turn is founded on a Babylonian incantation to Marduk. MacLeod Yearsley, in his very able work, "The Story of the Bible", renders the Kadish prayer as follows:

"Our father who art in heaven, be gracious to us, O Lord our God.

"Hallowed be thy name, and let the remembrance of thee be glorified in heaven above, and upon earth here below.

"Let thy kingdom reign over us, now and ever.

"The holy men of old said, Remit and forgive unto all men whatsoever they have done against thee;

"And lead us not into temptation, but deliver us from the evil thing;

"For thine is the kingdom, and thou shalt reign in glory, for ever and ever more."

The dogma of the Trinity is the most profound of all Christian doctrines. We are told that the Deity is composed of three distinct persons, and yet these three persons form only one God. There was a great controversy over this doctrine in the early Church, Athanasius maintaining that the Son was co-eternal with the Father, and Arius contending that it was quite impossible that a son could be as old as his father. The oldest trinity we know of, is that of ancient Egypt, which consisted of Osiris (Father), Horus (Son) and Isis (Mother). The Babylonian Trinity was composed of Anu (Lord of Heaven), Bel (Lord of Earth) and Ea (Lord of the Underworld). The Hindu Trinity comprised the following: Brahma (Creator), Vishnu (Preserver) and Siva (Destroyer). Sun-worship, it has been suggested, gave rise to the doctrine of the Trinity. Since living things cannot exist without sunlight, the ancients considered the sun as the Creator of life. Since life perishes when not nourished by the rays of the sun, that radiant orb was proclaimed the Preserver of life. And since too much sunlight withers and destroys living beings, the star of day was regarded as the Destroyer of life. Here we have the Sun as creator, preserver and destroyer, yet it is still only one Sun. This form of the trinity was known in ancient Egypt as Osiris (Creator), Horus (Preserver) and Set (Destroyer).

In the Gospel of St. John, Jesus is presented in the office of Judge of the Dead: "For the Father judgeth no man, but hath committed all judgment unto the Son." (John V., 22). Osiris enacted this role in the Egyptian religion. He is shown on the monuments, occupying the judgment seat, and holding the staff of authority and the crux ansata (cross with a handle). On his breast is a St. Andrew's cross. His throne is designed like a checker-board, the two colors representing the good and evil which come before him for judgment. The trial of the soul before Osiris in the Hall of Judgment is described in detail in the "Book of the Dead." According to the Hindus, Krishna will occupy the udgment seat on the last day.

Even the monastic and ecclesiastical organization of the early Christian Church was greatly influenced by pagan elements. There was a sect of religious monks, of pre-Christian origin, who had settlements in Judea, in the desert west of the Dead Sea, within a day's journey of Jerusalem and Bethlehem. These monks were known as the Essenes or Therapeutae, and they also had colonies in Egypt. It is held by some scholars that both Jesus and Paul were at one time members of this sacred brotherhood. It is believed that the Essenes were absorbed into the primitive Christian Church in the second century. "It is very likely," states Eusebius, "that the commentaries (Scriptures) which were among them (the Essenes) were the Gospels, and the works of the apostles, and certain expositions of the ancient prophets, such as partly that epistle unto the Hebrews, and also the other epistles of Paul do contain." (Ecclesiastical History," Book II., Ch. XVII). The moral and ethical precepts and practices of the Essenes are identical with those attributed to Jesus in the Gospels. "Their (the Essenes) parishes, churches, bishops, priests, deacons, festivals", asserts Sir Godfrey Higgins, "are all identically the same (as the Christians). They had Apostolic founders . . . scriptures divinely inspired . . . and the same order of performing public worship. They had missionary stations or colonies of their community established in Rome, Corinth, Galatia, Ephesus, Phillippi, Colosse and Thessalonica, precisely such, and in the same circumstances, as were those to whom St. Paul addressed his letters in those places."

Whether the author of this little essay has satisfactorily shown that Christianity existed before Christ, it is left for the reader to decide; but that paganism influenced Christianity deeply cannot be gainsaid. It is therefore fitting that we conclude with the words of that pioneer American Humanist, Rev. O. B. Frothingham, who wrote:

"Peter holds the keys of Janus. Moses wears the horns of Jove. Ceres, Cybele, Demeter assume new names as queen of Heaven, Star of the Sea, Maria Illuminatrix; Dionysus is St. Denis; Cosmos is St. Cosmo; Pluto and Proserpine resign their seats in the hall of final judgment to the Christ and his Mother . . No relic of Paganism was permitted to remain in its casket. The depositories were all ransacked. The shadowy hands of Egyptian priests placed the urn of holy water at the porch of the basilica, which stood ready to be converted into a temple. Priests of the most ancient faiths of Palestine, Assyria, Babylon, Thebes, Persia, were permitted to erect the altar at the point where the transverse beam of the cross meets the main steam. The hands that constructed the temple in cruciform shape had long become too attenuated to cast the faintest shadow. There Devaki with the infant Krishna, Maya with the babe Buddha, Juno with the child Mars, represented Mary with the child Jesus in her arms. Coarse emblems are not rejected; the Assyrian dove is a tender symbol of the Holy Ghost. The ragbags and toy boxes were explored. A bauble, which the Roman schoolboy had thrown away, was picked up and called an 'Agnus dei.' The musty wardrobes of forgotten hierarchies furnished costumes for the officers of the new prince. Alb and chasuble recalled the fashions of Numa's day. The cast-off purple habits and shoes of pagan emperors beautified the august persons of Christian popes. The cardinals must be contented with the robes once worn by senators. Zoroaster bound about the monks the girdle he invented as a protection against evil spirits, and clothed them in the frocks he had found convenient for his ritual. The pope thrust out his foot to be kissed, as Caligula, Heliogabalus, and Julius Caesar had thrust out theirs. Nothing came amiss to the faith that was to discharge henceforth the offices of spiritual impression." - "The Cradle of the Christ": a Study in Primitive Christianity, p. 179, New York, 1877. Cited by T. W. Doane in his "Bible Myths", pp. 399-400, New York, 1882).

ALLEN, GRANT..........................*The Evolution of the Idea of God*
BARNES HARRY ELMER ....*The Twilight of Christianity*
BONWICK. JAMES ....*Egyptian Belief and Modern Thought*
BROWN, Bishop W. M. ....*Science and History*
BUDGE, Sir WALLIS ....*The Gods of the Egyptians*
CARPENTER. EDWARD ....*Pagan and Christian Creeds*
DOANE, T. W. ....*Bible Myths*
DUPUIS, C. F. ....*The Origin of all Religious Worship*
FOOTE, G. W. ....*Bible Romances*
FORSYTH, DAVID ....*Psychology and Religion*
FRANK, HENRY ....*Jesus: A Modern Study*
FRAZER Sir J. G. ....*The Golden Bough*
FROTHINGHAM, O. B. ....*The Cradle of the Christ*
GAUVIN, MARSHALL J. ....*Fundamentals of Freethought*
GIBBON, EDWARD ....·...........*Decline and Fall of the Roman Empire*
GOULD, F. J. ....*A Concise History of Religion*
HARDING, A. M. ....*Astronomy*
HIGGINS, Sir GODFREY ....*The Anacalypsis*
MAHAFFY, J. P. .... *Prolegomena to Ancient History*
MASSEY, GERALD ....*Ancient Egypt*
    "   "   ....*Book of the Beginnings*
    "   "   ....*The Natural Genesis*
McCABE, JOSEPH ....*The Growth of Religion*
    "   "   ....*The Story of Religious Controversy*
PIKE, E. ROYSTON ....*Temple Bells*
POTTER, CHARLES FRANCIS ....*The Story of Religion*
READE, WINWOOD ....*The Veil of Isis*
REMSBURG, JOHN E. ....*The Christ*
RENAN, ERNEST ....*The Life of Jesus*
ROBERTSON. J. M. ....*Christianity and Mythology*
    "   "   "   ....*Pagan Christs*
    "   "   " ....*A Short History of Christianity*
RYLANDS, L. GORDON ....*The Christian Tradition*
    "   "   "   ....*Did Jesus Ever Live?*
    "   "   "   ....*The Evolution of Christianity*
SHARPE, SAMUEL ....*Egyptian Mythology and Egyptian Christianity*
TAYLOR, ROBERT ....*The Diegesis*
VIVIAN, PHILIP ....*The Churches and Modern Thought*
VOLNEY, C. F. ....*The Ruins of Empires*
WEIGALL, ARTHUR ....*The Paganism in Our Christianity*
WESTBROOK, R. B. ....*The Eliminator*
YEARSLEY, MACLEOD ....*The Story of the Bible*

Lightning Source UK Ltd.
Milton Keynes UK
UKHW010653040521
383094UK00004B/936